TEEN GIRLS Q&A

Copyright © 2018 Dr. Stem Sithembile Mahlatini.
All rights reserved.
ISBN: 978-1-7328275-4-7

All rights reserved. No part of this publication may be reproduced, stored in a retrieval system, or transmitted in any way by any means – electronic, mechanical, photocopy, recording, or otherwise – without the prior permissions of the copyright holder, except by reviewer who may quote brief passages in a review to be printed in magazine newspaper or by radio / TV announcement, as provided by USA copyright law. The author and the publisher will not be held responsible for any errors within the manuscript. All characters appearing in this work are fictitious. Any resemblance to real persons, living or dead is purely coincidental.

Written by: Dr. Stem Sithembile Mahlatini
drstem14@gmail.com | www.drstemspeaks.com
https://www.drstemmie.com/
Facebook: DrStem Mahlatini Twitter: DrStemahlatini
LinkedIn: Drstem Mahlatini Skype: Dr.Mahlatini

Foreword by: Dr.Stem Sithembile Mahlatini Cover Design by: Masimba Mukundinashe
Photo: EdPedi Photography Studio & Gardens
www.edpediphoto.com

Category: Historical, Biographical, Motivational, Inspirational, Educational and Empowerment
Library of Congress Cataloging-in-Publication Data
Printed in the USA

TEEN GIRLS Q&A

There are so many reasons why I have so much confidence in you. When I work or write for teenagers, I see greatness, I see inner courage, inner and outer beauty like no one else. I see determination to make it through these teen years, no matter what. I believe in you.

I hope the information and answers I have in this book will guide you to make choices that will serve you best. It is not easy to be a teenager today because of all the challenges and choices you face at times. Be encouraged, never let failures, doubts, drugs, alcohol, negative people and insecurities stop you from achieving your dreams.

Dr. Stem—Be Encouraged

Contents

1. **WELCOME TO TEENAGE LIFE** 11

   WHY IS MY BODY IS CHANGING? 13
   - Should I Diet? 14
   - What About My Skin? 15
   - Self-Image 16

2. **WHAT ABOUT MY MENSTRUAL CYCLE?** 21
   - Tips for Embracing My Changing Body 25
   - Why Is My Body Changing? Scenario 27
   - Why Is My Body Changing? Self-Reflection 28
   - Why Is My Body Changing? Assignment 30

3. **WHY ARE MY EMOTIONS CHANGING?** 33
   - Depression and Suicide 34
   - Stress, Anxiety and Cutting 35
   - Why Are My Emotions Changing? Scenario 37
   - Why Are My Emotions Changing? Self-Reflection 39
   - Why Are My Emotions Changing? Assignment 41

4. **PEER PRESSURE: HOW DO I DEAL WITH WHAT'S TRENDING?** 45
   - Drugs 47
   - Alcohol 50
   - Casual Dating and Sex 52
     - Sexually Transmitted Diseases (STDs) 55
     - Teenage Pregnancy 56
     - Sexting 57

5. **WHAT ABOUT MY FRIENDS?** 59
   Peer Pressure: How do I deal with What's Trending?
   Scenario I 61
   Peer Pressure: How Do I Deal with What's Trending?
   Scenario II 64
   Peer Pressure: How Do I Deal with What's Trending?
   Self-Reflection 66
   Peer Pressure: How Do I Deal with What's Trending?
   Self-Reflection II 68
   Peer Pressure: How Do I Deal with What's Trending?
   Assignment 70

6. **SOCIAL MEDIA: WHAT'S THE BIG DEAL?** 73
   Cyber Bullying 75
   Social Media: What's the Big Deal? **Scenario I** 77
   Social Media: What's the Big Deal? **Scenario II** 78
   Social Media: What's the Big Deal? Self-Reflection 80
   Social Media: What's the Big Deal? Assignment 82

7. **Dating, Love and Committed Relationships: What Does it All Mean?** 85
   Dating: The Point of It All 85
   What If I'm Asked Out on A Date? 87
   Where Should We Go? 88
   What If I'm Not Interested? 88
   What If I'm Uncomfortable with Dating? 89
   What If My Parents and I Don't See Eye to Eye About Dating 89
   What Is Love? 91
   What Is A Committed Relationship? 94
   Dealing with Heartbreak? 94

Dating, Love and Committed Relationships: What Does It All Mean? **Scenario I**..96

Dating, Love and Committed Relationships: What Does It All Mean? **Scenario II**..98

Dating, Love and Committed Relationships: What Does It All Mean? **Scenario III**..100

Dating, Love and Committed Relationships: What Does It All Mean? **Self-Reflection**..102

Dating, Love and Committed Relationships: What Does It All Mean? **Assignment**..104

8. **WHAT IF I'M NOT SURE ABOUT MY SEXUAL ORIENTATION?**.. **107**

9. **HOW DO I DEAL WITH MY PARENTS DIVORCE**.................. **109**

10. **HOW DO I BUILD RELATIONSHIPS WITH MY PARENTS AND MENTORS**..**117**

    How Do I Build Relationships with My Parents and Mentors? **Scenario**..120

    How Do I Build Relationships with My Parents and Mentors? **Self Reflection**..122

    How Do I Build Relationships with My Parents and Mentors? **Assignment**..124

11. **SETTING PERSONAL GOALS**..**127**

    What Is A Personal Goal?..127

    Being Accountable for Your Goals..128

    Tips for Achieving Your Goals..130

    Setting Personal Goals: **Scenario**..132

    Setting Personal Goals: **Self-Reflection**..134

    Setting Personal Goals: **Assignment**..136

12. **AFFIRMATIONAL THOUGHTS AND NEXT STEPS**..................**138**

APPENDIX:

Doses of Motivation & Encouragement..140
About the Author..141
Let's Connect... 142
Training, Individual and Group Life Coaching...............................143

Dr. Stem
Helping Teens Excel

TEEN GIRLS Q&A

Be *Original* Encouraged

You can **never make** the **same mistake twice** because the second time you make it, it's not a mistake, it's a choice.

Being a teenager is an amazing time and a hard time. It's when you make your best friends - I have girls who will never leave my heart and I still talk to. You get the best and the worst as a teen. You have the best friendships and the worst heartbreaks.

- Sophia Bush

Welcome to Teenage Life!

You're officially a TEEN! How do you know?

Aside from your age, you're noticing all sorts of changes—physically, emotionally, and even in the way you see the world. You might also be noticing these same changes in your friends.

Not to mention, the questions from your parents are becoming weirder by the minute.

Don't worry! We're here to talk about all of it. But, first, you should know that the teenage phase you're experiencing now will equip you for adulthood. That's why every decision you make is important. You won't always get it all right, but that's ok.

What's important is that you're equipped with knowledge, you understand who you are, set goals for yourself, and surround yourself with people who love you and want you to succeed.

As we explore what it means to be a teenager, you should also know there's no question that should be off limits and no situation you should face alone. In fact, this book was written to make sure you have answers to your questions and to keep you company along your journey. You'll have the opportunity to jot down your thoughts, questions and participate in some cool exercises.

An important part of dating is communicating. We communicate by sharing our thoughts, ideas, and feelings. We enjoy being with someone when we have an easy time communicating or when we have a lot to talk about.
- John Bytheway

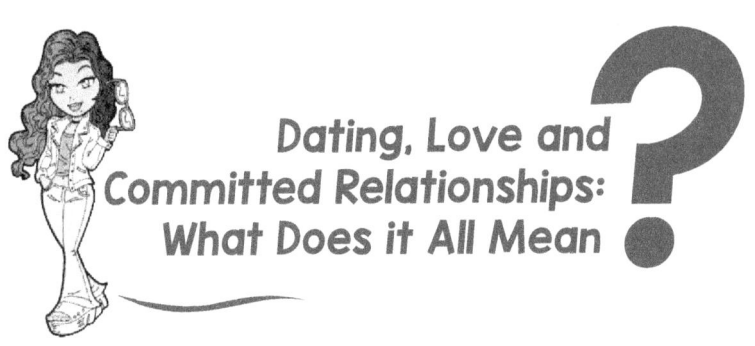

Dating, Love and Committed Relationships: What Does it All Mean?

Hormones are responsible for your changing body.

Now that you're a teen, your brain releases a special hormone called gonadotropin-releasing hormone, also known as GnRH. Simply put, when this hormone reaches the pituitary gland, which is the gland just under your brain, the hormones responsible for puberty kick in.

For girls, this means tons of estrogen and progesterone. These hormones are responsible for many of the physical and emotional changes you're experiencing.

You might notice that certain areas of your body are filling out more. For example, you might not be able to get away with not wearing a bra anymore or that you've outgrown your current bra size. Maybe your jeans fit a little tighter in the hip and butt area.

Don't panic— these types of changes are completely normal during puberty.

Should I Diet?

Struggling with weight is not uncommon.

Many teens girls struggle with whether or not dieting is a healthy option if they experience weight gain. Some take dieting too far and decide not to eat at all. However, depriving your body of the nutrients it needs is never a good idea. In fact, your body needs all of the healthy nutrients it can get during this stage.

On the other hand, some teens go through great lengths to put weight on to achieve a certain shape or figure. This might lead to unhealthy eating practices. Unless your doctor tells you to change your diet in any way, don't attempt any "fad" diets because they appear to be popular.

Weight gain during puberty is completely normal, and so is weight loss. What's most important is that you're healthy. This means including healthy foods in your normal diet and being physically active.

Eating well and exercising at least 30 minutes a day not only improves your health, but makes you feel great!

What About My Skin?

Your skin is no exception to hormonal changes.

You might have noticed that even your face gets a little bit of the puberty action because episodes of acne make it harder to keep your skin clear. Acne is also triggered by your changing hormones and causes your sebaceous glands, which are your oil glands, to enlarge and overproduce oil.

This causes your skin to become inflamed and can result in blemishes and pimples. Acne can also present itself on the shoulders, back, neck, chest and upper arms. If you can't seem to get your acne under control, talk to your parents or one of your mentors so that they can help you identify the best solution for your skin.

A few tips for maintaining clear skin include, drinking plenty of water, washing and moisturizing your face once or twice daily, using mild cleansers without fragrances that irritate your skin, and applying less makeup so that your skin can breathe. your health, but makes you feel great!

What About My Self Image?

Self-image is the way you see yourself.

This includes how you look, and even how you perceive your personality. Teen girls are especially concerned about their physical image at this stage. You might be paying more attention to your size, your height, the color of your hair, and even the style of your clothes.

Many teen girls try to mimic what they see on television to try to fit in or be noticed.

Here are tips to help Boost your self-image which will result in higher self confidence.

- ***Be nice to yourself***
  That little voice that tells you says you are not good enough, you are not worthy tends to be the voice that lets you judge yourself harshly at times. So make it a point to like yourself, love who you are and believe you have everything it takes to be the best you. A good rule of thumb is to speak to yourself in the same way that you'd speak to other people you admire.

- ***Do You***
  Comparing yourself to other people is a sure-fire way to start feeling yikes and second best. Try to focus on

your own strengths, goals and achievements, rather than measuring comparing yourself negatively against other people

- ***Exercise and Get Involved***
  Exercise is a great way to increase your self-confidence and motivation. Exercising makes you look and feel good, so it is a win-win situation.

- **Be The Best Version of Yourself**
  Nobody's perfect. Always strive to be the best version of yourself, but it's also important to accept that perfection is an unrealistic goal.

- **Be The Best Version of Yourself**
  Nobody's perfect. Always strive to be the best version of yourself, but it's also important to accept that perfection is an unrealistic goal.

- **Mistakes Help You Grow**
  Remember that everyone makes mistakes. You've got to make mistakes in order to learn and grow, so try not to beat yourself up if you make mistakes.

  Learn and avoid making the same mistake twice. Everyone's been there.

- **Be In Control**
  Focus on what you can change. It's easy to get hung up on all the things that are out of your control, but it won't achieve much. Instead, try to focus your energy on identifying the things that are within your control and seeing what you can do about them. When you think you can, you will. When you think you can't then you won't. Be in control of your thoughts, actions and the choices you make.

- **Do what makes you happy**
  If you spend time doing the things you enjoy, you're more likely to think positively. Try to hang around positive friends who are doing well or better than you so that you can aim high.

- **Celebrate Your Wins**
  Celebrate yourself even if it is the small stuff, like getting up on time, being on school on time and when you pass a test or get a good passing grade. Even when you don't feel like no one is celebrating your achievement, celebrate you. Tell yourself well done, brag, eat ice cream or whatever you desire and can afford.

- **Volunteer**
  Being helpful and considerate to other people will certainly boost their mood, but it'll also make you feel pretty good about yourself.

- **Surround yourself with a supportive people**
  Most states, countries have programs where teenagers can earn volunteer hours towards their school credits. Volunteering also gives you a sense of achievement when you help another person when you volunteer. Some teenagers actually find their career choice through volunteer work. Surround yourself with people who make you feel good about yourself and avoid those who tend to trigger your negative thinking, even in volunteer situations.

- **Spruce up your appearance**
  Take time for proper grooming and dressing. Wear clean, ironed clothes, use deodorant and perfume (if you can), otherwise you can use just deodorant.
  Shower and curl your hair, or tie it nicely daily. Brush Your teeth. Wash and Comb your hair. When you feel clean you feel more confident.

- **What others think about your personality might also matter to you.**

It's common for teens to become concerned about whether or not people like them. You might be wondering if you're cool enough or if your peers think you're weird or "nerdy". What's important is that you always remain true to who you are.

Don't ever try act differently to please other people. It's not worth the effort to create an image of yourself just to try to fit in. It's much easier to be your natural self. In fact, being uniquely you is what makes you special. You're not meant to be like anyone else, you're meant to be YOU! Those who are meant to be in your life will appreciate you just for who you are.

We either make ourselves miserable or we make ourselves strong. The amount of work is the same. **-Carlos Castenada**

What About My Menstrual Cycle?

By now, you might have already experienced your menstrual cycle, also known as your "period".

If you haven't experienced it yet, it will be here before you know it. Menstruating is nothing to be afraid of. In fact, it's completely healthy and natural. Your menstrual cycle is your body's way of preparing for a pregnancy each month. A woman's cycle typically lasts anywhere between 21 to 45 days. This doesn't mean you'll actually bleed this number of days. Menstrual bleeding typically lasts no more than a week.

Menstrual bleeding can vary from person to person.

You might be wondering how long your menstrual bleeding should last. Although menstrual bleeding typically lasts for about a week, it is possible for the number of days to vary from month to month. It is also possible to experience lighter or heavier flows from month to month.

While some teens experience a regular cycle that allows them to anticipate when their menstrual bleeding will begin, others experience irregular cycles which makes it harder to pinpoint when their menstrual bleeding will begin. You might also experience different comfort levels with different menstrual or feminine products.

Don't be discouraged. There are plenty of menstrual products out there. Take your time to find products that suit your needs in terms of comfort and flow.

Your cycle is counted from the first day of one period to the first day of the next period.

About halfway through your cycle, your ovaries release an egg which travels down your fallopian tubes to be fertilized by a sperm. Your hormones begin to rise and the lining in your uterus begins to thicken. This is a process known as ovulation.

Pregnancy happens if the egg is fertilized by a man's sperm and attaches to the woman's uterine wall. If the egg is not fertilized, it will break apart. This causes your hormone levels to drop and the thickened lining of the uterus to "melt away". When this happens, the lining exits your body in the form of blood. Your body repeats this process every month.

Be patient while your cycles run their course.

Even though menstrual cycles can sometimes be uncomfortable and make you irritable, they are designed to naturally cleanse your body of the uterine lining that thickens every month in preparation for pregnancy.
If you decide to have children once you've entered into a committed relationship and, ultimately, marriage, your body will have had lots of practice ovulating.

Remember, having a menstrual cycle is completely natural. However, if you experience unbearable pain or abnormally heavy bleeding, bring it to the attention of your parent, school nurse, teacher or mentor so that it can be discussed with your doctor.

Also, track the start of your menstrual cycles from one month to next and make note of any major changes.

In every aspect of life, have a game plan, and then do your best to achieve it. -Alan Kulwicki

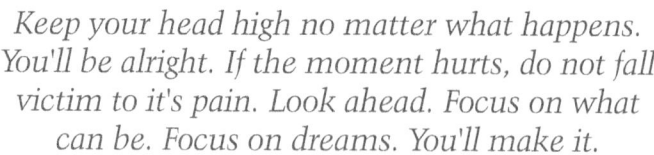

Keep your head high no matter what happens. You'll be alright. If the moment hurts, do not fall victim to it's pain. Look ahead. Focus on what can be. Focus on dreams. You'll make it.

Tips For Embracing My Changing Body

Embrace Your Changing Body

None of the changes your body is experiencing make you any less beautiful! The fact that your body is maturing is beautiful in itself.

So, what can you do about all of these physical changes? Here are a few tips.

- Try wearing clothing that you feel comfortable in. Whether you enjoy walking around the mall with your friends or actively playing sports, shop for undergarments (i.e., bras, underwear) that feel good on. Don't settle on a bra or underwear simply because it looks cute.

- Eat healthy and exercise at least 30 minutes a day.

- Try not to overcompensate for your acne with makeup. Too much makeup can actually clog your pores. What your skin needs most is oxygen and water.

- Get plenty of rest. Being well rested improves your overall mood.

- Remind yourself of how beautiful you are. Focus on the things you love about yourself. Try not be get distracted by anything else.

 *If people are trying to bring you down, it only means you are above them.*
-unknown

Why is My Body Changing? -Scenario:

- Jessica is getting prepared for her best friend's birthday party. She notices her favorite pair of jeans don't slide on as easily as they used to. She also notices two pimples that have appeared on her forehead overnight and is feeling a little "crampy". You see Jessica at the party and notice she's not eating anything. She also has on more makeup than normal and appears to be uncomfortable.

What advice would you give Jessica based on what you know about the changes her body might be going through?

_____
_____
_____
_____
_____
_____
_____
_____
_____
_____

Why is My Body Changing? -Self Reflection:

- *What changes have you noticed about your body? How does this make you feel?*

- *What are some things can you do to remind yourself of your beauty and remain comfortable, despite the changes your body may be going through?*

Your Answer Here....

Why is My Body Changing? -Assignment:

- *Commit to doing at least one of the things you listed to remind yourself of your beauty every day for the rest of this week. Then, describe how doing this made you feel. You can do this by using words or a drawing.*

Your Answer Here....
_____

_____

_____

_____

_____

_____

_____

_____

_____

_____

_____

_____

Be who you are and say what you feel, because those who mind don't matter and those who matter don't mind.
Dr Seuss

Why Are My Emotions Changing?

Puberty affects your emotions.

Do you find yourself feeling happy then suddenly sad or frustrated at times for no apparent reason?

Some may even say that your emotions are "up" and "down". That's because those same hormones that affect your body physically also affect you emotionally. That's right—estrogen and progesterone are also affecting your mood!

Not to worry, most teen girls experience frequent changes in mood as their bodies become flooded with hormones. You might also hear this referred to as mood swings.

If mood swings make you uncomfortable, try to avoid things that irritate you. For example, don't spend too much time on social media if the posts and comments that come across your feed upset you often. Likewise, don't watch television shows or listen to music that make you feel sad or frustrated.

Make it a point to do things that naturally improve your mood instead, such as listening to positive music, writing, drawing, jogging or helping others in need.

Depression & Suicide

Pay attention to how you're feeling.

If it seems none of the things that once made you happy no longer interest you, or you consistently feel sad, crying for no reason, not feeling like getting up or doing anything, alone or withdrawn, you might be suffering from depression.

Other symptoms might include a loss of appetite, wanting to sleep more often, or even wanting to end your life.

If you ever experience suicidal thoughts, contact someone right away!

This can be one of your parents, nurse, teacher a mentor or a close friend.

The National Suicide Hotline is also a resource that is available to you with trained professionals who are ready to help 24 hours a day at 1-800-273-8255, the USA.

Nothing is worth taking your own life! No matter how bad things may seem to get or how bad you might feel, there is always something better ahead for you. Don't rob yourself of the great life you have to live ahead because of where you are temporarily. Get help! There's no need to be ashamed or embarrassed. There are many professionals out there who are trained and ready to help you through depression and will meet you right where you are.

Stress, Anxiety and Cutting.

Many of the same symptoms described for depression can also present themselves if you are experiencing anxiety or high stress. Being anxious is normal when faced with danger, but the constant feeling of anxiety is not healthy.

Pay attention to how you're feeling.

This might include feelings of nervousness or feeling jittery. It can also include feelings of intense sadness, frustration, or anger. Some teens resort to cutting to take their minds off of their problems or release their tension and stress.

However, cutting will only temporarily distract you from your problems, not eliminate them. This can also turn into a habit that you continue into adulthood and leave you with permanent scars. Cutting can also be life-threatening. Accidentally cutting a vein can cause you to bleed out rapidly, lose consciousness and die.

It is important not to ignore feelings of depression, anxiety or high stress. Be sure to bring these feelings to the attention of your parents or mentor so that they can get you get the help that you need. Even if you're not sure about the feelings you're experiencing, don't be embarrassed to talk about how you feel. Communicate, communicate, communicate!

Never chase love, affection or attention. If it isn't given freely by another person, it isn't worth having.

Why Are My Emotions Changing? - Scenario:

Jessica normally volunteers to take the lead on every class project. You like doing school projects with Jessica because she's smart and fun to work with, just like you. Lately, you notice she hasn't volunteered to lead anything and she's not her normal, bubbly self. You also noticed she didn't score at the top of the class during your last major test. Jessica tells you she's not feeling herself.

What advice would you give Jessica?

_____
_____
_____
_____
_____
_____
_____
_____
_____
_____
_____
_____
_____

Why Are My Emotions Changing?

- What are some things that make you feel irritable or frustrated?

- What are some things that naturally brighten up your mood?

- Can you think of a time when you didn't feel like yourself, no matter how hard you tried? **If this feeling is ongoing, share this with your parent or mentor.**

_____
_____
_____
_____
_____
_____
_____
_____
_____
_____
_____
_____

Why Are My Emotions Changing? - Assignment:

- Make a list of at least 5 things or activities that make you irritable. Commit to eliminating at least one of those things for the rest of the week. Write down how eliminating this one thing has made you feel once the week is over.

___
___
___
___
___
___
___
___
___
___
___
___
___
___
___
___

The 3 C's in life:
Choice, Chance, Change
You must make the choice, take the Chance if you want anything in your life to Change.

PEER PRESSURE: How Do I Deal With What's Trending

Aside from all of the hormones you're experiencing, you may have noticed you're under a lot of pressure lately—pressure from your parents, teachers, and especially your friends. Most times what feels like pressure coming from your parents and loved ones is actually just their desire to see you succeed because they love you.

If you feel that pressure from your loved ones is overwhelming, be sure to let them know. It's important that you work on your approaches to communicate with one another effectively together.

Perhaps the most dangerous type of pressure is the type that comes from your friends.

Everything seems to be trending— even thing's you're not comfortable with, but that doesn't stop your friends from trying to convince you to "try it". This is what we call peer pressure. Peer pressure is basically a feeling that you must do certain things or behave a certain way because your friends make it appear as though you're somehow missing out or not part of the "in crowd". Sometimes, this pressure comes from so- called friends who aren't even closest to you.

They might be distance classmates or friends of friends. They might seem to have it all together from afar, but they typically feed off of attention or their popularity to compensate for their insecurities.

 *Be strong enough to stand alone. Smart enough to know when you need help, and brave enough to ask for it.*

Drugs

Using drugs is never a good idea.

Many teens participate in drug use because it seems like something fun to do. Some do it because they want people around them to think that they're "down" or to try to fit in. Others do it in secret because they think it will help them take away their emotional pain or feel better about themselves. These are all false assumptions. In fact, using drugs is a sign that a person is too weak to be themselves; they need something to latch onto to feel like they're a part of something. It's also a sign that they're unable to deal with their emotions without depending on a substance. This makes them more susceptible to drug addiction.

Taking drugs will not eliminate a person's emotional pain.

At best, it will temporarily distract a person from their pain. This fleeting distraction leads them to depend on the drug over and over again which leads to drug dependence, also known as drug addiction.
This means, eventually, their bodies begin to depend on the drug to the point where they can't function without out. There is no fun in drug addiction because it takes over a person's entire life. They lose their focus and their sense of self. For a teen, this means losing friends, dropping out

of school, losing the trust of their parents and loved ones, and even their life.

There's no such thing as a safe drug.

There's nothing trendy or safe about a drug because of its name or popularity. One of the most common traps that teens fall into is believing that a drug isn't harmful because of its trendy name. These days, drugs aren't called "drugs" anymore. They have fun, cute names that make them appear harmless.

However, what most teens don't realize is that all drugs have negative effects on their brain and bodies.

Even more dangerous, most teens don't know what they're actually consuming when they take what they think is a "harmless drug". For example, marijuana, which has negative effects of its own, can have even worse effects if laced with other lethal drugs, such as cocaine.

Drugs don't come with instructions, ingredients or warning labels. There's simply no way of knowing what you're really putting into your body. No matter what anyone tells you, there is no such thing as a safe drug.

Drugs impact the circuits in your brain. They especially affect what's called your limbic system by causing dangerously large amounts of dopamine to flood your system. This causes a shift in the way that your brain functions and can prevent you from thinking clearly. Drug use can also lead to lung and heart disease overtime. Some drugs are even made of deadly chemicals that can send you into a coma or cause your heart to stop immediately upon taking them.

Prescription drugs are no exception.

Another dangerous misconception is that taking a prescription drugs is safer than taking drugs that aren't prescribed by a doctor. This is false! Even drugs prescribed by a doctor can be dangerous if the drug was not prescribed for you or if it's not taken according to the doctor's orders.

For example, you should never take an opioid (or pain pill) that has been prescribed to a family member or a friend. Improper dosage of these drugs can lead to death. Even if a certain medication is prescribed to you by a doctor, you should never take more than the dosage instructed.

No matter how harmless trying a drug might seem, remember that your brain can be altered, and that you can easily become addicted. Also, some drugs can lead to immediate death, even after one try.

If your friends are pressuring you to try any type of drug, let your parent or mentor know because their lives could be in danger

Alcohol

Maybe you have no intention of doing drugs but your friends try to convince you that alcohol is ok. They're wrong! In fact, alcohol can have many of the same negative effects on your brain and body as drugs.

You don't need alcohol to fit in or have fun.

Like drugs, many teens think that drinking alcohol makes them appear more mature or helps them to fit in. There's also a misconception that alcohol will enhance their ability to have fun. What alcohol actually does is reduce your brain's ability to make sound decisions, which makes it harder for your conscious to kick in when it needs to.

Not being able to think clearly can be very dangerous! You can find yourself somewhere unconscious or have a dangerous fall. You might also subject yourself to having someone

taking advantage of you or date rape if you're not able to think clearly.

You can actually enjoy yourself more when your mind isn't clouded. Having "clean" fun also prevents you from experiencing awful side effects caused by drinking alcohol, such as dizziness, nausea and vomiting. You might even be able to save a life if you're in a situation where you're the only person in the group who is not intoxicated with alcohol because you're able to think clearly and seek help.

Drinking alcohol can lead to addiction and poor health.

Drinking can especially be harmful to teens because their brains are still developing. In fact, this is considered a critical stage of development for what is required of the brain as an adult, such as critical thinking and decision-making.

Teenage drinking can lead to brain damage which can cause memory loss or the loss of motor skills. Drinking can also lead to liver and other chronic diseases over time. Teens who begin drinking before the age of 21 are also much more likely to develop alcohol addiction.

When someone judges you, it isn't actually about you. It's about them and their own insecurities, and needs.

Casual Dating and Sex

Casual dating and sex is perhaps one of the biggest forms of peer pressure you might experience as a teen. However, there's nothing casual about dating when it involves sex. Many teens girls feel that having sex will make them more popular or more appealing to guys. You might experience feeling pressured by some of your girlfriends to have sex as something fun to do. They might even describe it as "not a big deal".

This pressure can be even worse if it's coming from a guy directly, especially if it's a guy that you like.

Sex is more than a feeling.

At this stage, every teenager wants to feel loved and accepted. The idea of a cute guy wanting to be intimate with you might make you feel incredibly desirable. You might even feel butterflies or unusually excited. This might make believe that you have a physical or emotional connection.

But, remember, the hormones that are responsible for puberty affect how you feel physically and emotionally. Never make the decision to engage in sexual activity with anyone because of how they make you feel. Most times, it's just your hormones running their course.

Sex is not just about fun and games.

The truth is, sex is not just a fun thing to do or something that makes you feel good. It's a form of bonding that has long-lasting effects. Did you know that your brain actually releases a chemical called oxytocin when having sex, which is the same chemical released when mothers breastfeed their babies to help them bond?

That's how powerful oxytocin is. So, the idea that you can just have sex for the fun of it is completely false! It's a lot more complicated than that.

Sex affects you emotionally.

it can be rather hard to emotionally distance yourself from a guy you've had sex with, especially for girls. What you think might be fun could leave you feeling rejected and empty in the long run, which can really harm your self-esteem.

Many girls find themselves having sex because they have low self-esteem to begin with. They have a false hope that being wanted by a guy, even if only for her body, will make them feel better about themselves. Most times, this is because there are trying to fill a void that impacts their self-esteem.

For example, not having both parents in the home or being abused and neglected could all result in voids that make the idea of someone wanting to have sex with them seem appealing.

However, like drugs and alcohol, sex is only a temporary distraction from a larger problem. Becoming addicted to sexual activity is also very possible.

Sex does not equal love.

It is important to realize that guys experience many of these same pressures. They're being pressured by their friends to have sex to prove their "manhood" and have voids to fill of their own. Not to mention, they're also being flooded with hormones.

So, it is highly unlikely that a guy is interested in having sex with you because he's deeply in love and plans to be with you for the rest of his life. Like you, he's still growing and has a lot of maturing to do. Having sex with him will not cause him to fall in love with you.

If a guy tries to convince you that the only way he'll remain interested in you is if you have sex with him, he's not worth being in a relationship with.

A guy who truly cares about you will respect you enough to not pressure you into doing anything you're uncomfortable with.

Sexually Transmitted Diseases (STDs)

Some teens believe they can keep their emotions under control by having "casual" sex. If you have sex for fun without getting your emotions involved, no one can get hurt, right? Wrong! Getting involved with more people only increases your risk of being hurt, both emotionally and physically. What you might think will lead to occasional pleasure and fun could actually lead to a lifetime of disaster, especially if you contract a sexually transmitted disease (STD) or become pregnant.

STDs have long-term effects. The most common forms of STDs are chlamydia, gonorrhea, genital herpes, human papillomavirus (HPV), syphilis and HIV. Although chlamydia and gonorrhea are treatable, they aren't treated overnight, and they can have long-term effects later in adulthood.

Both of these infections can cause unpleasant orders, nasty vaginal discharges, and lots of itching and swelling in the vaginal area. Over time, these infections can lead to cervical cancer or complications with becoming pregnant when you're ready.

HIV, genital herpes and HIV are not curable. If you contract any of these viruses, they remain with you for the rest of your life.

No form of sexual activity or protection is 100% safe. Some of your friends might try to convince you that you're safe from these infections as long as you use protection, such as a condom. They might even try to convince you that engaging in other forms of sexual activity, such as oral sex, is safer. However, none of this is true. STDs are spread through the exchange of bodily fluid.

Oral sex certainly presents the opportunity for the exchange of fluid. Likewise, condoms are not 100% guaranteed to prevent leakage of bodily fluid. Bodily fluid isn't the only thing to be concerned about. Genital herpes can be contracted simply through skin to skin contact—no fluid necessary.

So, think twice before deciding to engage in any type of sexual activity.

Teenage Pregnancy

Aside from contracting a STD, having sex can lead to an unplanned pregnancy. Having a baby as a teen comes with a great deal of responsibility and can lead to extremely high levels of stress. As a pregnant teen, you'd be responsible for supporting both you and your growing baby.

This means dealing with your own changing hormones, meeting the demands of nurturing a baby inside of the wound, and nurturing and providing for your baby after birth.

Babies require lots of time, money and attention, which will require you to spend a lot less time, money and attention on the things you currently enjoy. It is very common for teen mothers to struggle with finishing school. Teen mothers also commonly struggle with what's called post-partum depression, which is a type of depression that presents itself after a woman delivers her baby.

If you think you might already be pregnant, talk to a parent or mentor you trust right away.

Pregnancy can affect your emotions and your health, so it's important to surround yourself with a strong support system.

Sexting

Sexting is never a good alternative to having sex.

Sexting involves taking and sending explicit pictures or messages to someone. You might have friends who try to convince you that sexting is ok because you're not actually engaging in the act. However, sexting is never ok. Not only does it entice the person who's receiving these texts and images to engage in sexual activity, it also puts the privacy of the person who sends the messages in great danger.

Sexting jeopardizes privacy and can be illegal.

Once a "sext" is in the hands of the person who received it, the content of the "sext" is subject to being shared with anyone, anywhere. This might mean that the messages are forwarded to other people's phones or even circulated on the internet!

Sending sexual images to minors is also against the law. Some states have even begun prosecuting minors for child pornography or felony obscenity. If you ever receive a "sext", be sure to make a parent or mentor aware so that they can protect you.

You do not have to "sext" to show get anyone's attention or to prove your interest in them. Remember, anyone who pressures you to do anything that is uncomfortable to you to prove your interest in them only has their best interest in mind.

No one sees how much you do for them, they only see what you don't do.

What About My Friends?

Your friends impact your decisions.

Even if you've never engaged in any of the activities already described, you might have friends who are actively engaged in these activities. This might make engaging in unsafe behavior more tempting. It can also be hard knowing that they're engaged in activities that could negatively impact their lives.

So, what do you do about it? You can try talking to them about the effects of their behavior based on the knowledge you've gained. You can also let them know that you're concerned about them because you care. It is also best to share what you know about their behavior with a trusted adult to prevent them from harm.

Looking out for each other's best interest is what real friends are for.

It can be hard to talk to someone about a friend's behavior because you don't want to betray your friend's trust. Your friend might even be upset with you for a while for sharing what they consider is their personal business. However, their health and safety are what's most important.

Unfortunately, friends sometimes have a hard time understanding why you would want them to stop doing certain things that were once okay with. They might take it personally and feel that you no longer want to hang out with them. They might even accuse you of being judgmental or threaten to no longer remain friends with you if you don't turn a blind eye.

Although this can be hurtful, pretending that you're okay with their behavior can actually hurt them more. It is better to distance yourself from a friend than to put your life or theirs in danger.

Friends hold one another accountable.

Perhaps both you and your friend have already engaged in some of these activities together. It's not too late to change this behavior for either of you. In fact, you can share with your friend that you want to work on eliminating these activities from your life and welcome them to join you.

This will allow you to support one another and hold one another accountable. Because your brain is still maturing, it is important that you involve a responsible adult in your accountability journey because they have the level of maturity that is necessary to help you through temptation and difficult decisions

Peer Pressure: How Do I Deal With What's Trending? - Scenario II:

You've been invited to a classmate's party. Halfway through the party, a group of friends ask you to go with them to the bathroom. When you get there, they try to convince you to drink some alcohol that they've mixed with some pills. They tell you that it's safe because they do it all the time. They also tell you it will help you to loosen up so that you can have more fun. You're the only person in the bathroom who hasn't tried the drink mixed with pills. How does this make you feel?

What do you do?

_____
_____
_____
_____
_____
_____
_____
_____
_____
_____

Peer Pressure: How Do I Deal With What's Trending? - Scenario II:

A guy that you really like tells you he's into you and asks you if you've ever had sex. You tell him no and he begins to laugh. He tells you that he doesn't date girls who can't prove to him that they're really into him. He promises to be gentle and not to tell anyone. He finds it hard to believe that you're into him if you're not willing to try anything with him at all. You talk to your girlfriends about it and they tell you how lucky you are that he likes you because so many other girls are into him. He even begins to send you sexually explicit text messages.

What do you do?

_____

_____

_____

_____

_____

_____

_____

_____

_____

Peer Pressure: How Do I Deal With What's Trending? - Self-Reflection

- *Have you ever been pressured to take drugs or drink alcohol? How did it make you feel? How did you handle it? How would you handle it differently?*

- *Have you ever been pressured to have sex? How did it make you feel? How did you handle it? How would you handle it differently?*

_____
_____
_____
_____
_____
_____
_____
_____
_____
_____
_____
_____

Peer Pressure: How Do I Deal With What's Trending? - Self-Reflection II:

A guy that you really like tells you he's into you and asks you if you've ever had sex. You tell him no and he begins to laugh. He tells you that he doesn't date girls who can't prove to him that they're really into him. He promises to be gentle and not to tell anyone. He finds it hard to believe that you're into him if you're not willing to try anything with him at all. You talk to your girlfriends about it and they tell you how lucky you are that he likes you because so many other girls are into him. He even begins to send you sexually explicit text messages.

What do you do?

_____

_____

_____

_____

_____

_____

_____

_____

_____

Peer Pressure: How Do I Deal With What's Trending? - Assignment:

Make a list of the things your peers pressure you to do most. Write down the name of the peer/friend next to each item who pressures you most. Talk to each peer/friend associated with each item on your list about the pressure they are causing you by the end of the week.

If you want to be happy, you have to be happy on purpose. When you wake up you can't just wait to see what kind of day you'll gave. You have to decide what kind of day you'll have.
Joel Osteen

Social Media What's The BIG Deal?

Social media is everywhere.

Posts, likes, chats and follows seem to run the world. They determine the clothes we wear, the music we listen to, what we watch on television, and what we purchase in stores or online. In fact, companies of all sizes flood social media with their products and services because they know it's where they'll find the majority of their consumers, especially teens.

Social media influences our interests and actions.

It's where we get our news from and "inside scoop" into the lives of other people. We often times decide who we want to connect to, based on the interests and stories of those on social media and the attention they receive.

Regardless of how often you view social media, you are being influenced by its content. For example, it might influence how you feel about politics or even your own sense of fashion.

Social media can be dangerous.

Though social media can be a positive place for networking and sharing, you should always be mindful of the people you choose to follow and allow to follow you. Unfortunately, many people use social media to gather information on you and lure you into scams.

Predators sometimes use social media to start conversations with teen girls and build their trust so that they can eventually take advantage of them.

Never agree to meet a stranger who tries to befriend you on social media.

 *the world is gonna judge you no matter what you do. So live your way the best way you can.*

Cyber Bullying?

Social media is often used as a tool for cyber bullying.

Unfortunately, many people use social media to embarrass, harass or threaten others. This is called cyber bullying. Cyber bullying can also happen over text messages or email. If you haven't experienced cyber bullying before, you might be wondering how it is possible to be bullied by someone who you can't see or hear.

Reading negative words that target you can cause you to internalize them. Threatening words can also cause anxiety and fear.

Cyber bullying can have harmful emotional effects.

If you're affected by cyber bullying frequently or over a long period of time, you can develop anxiety, stress and even depression. In fact, teens who experience high incidences of cyber bullying also have higher incidences of suicidal thoughts or attempts.

If you're experiencing threats or harassing comments by text or social media, it's important to share this information with a parent of mentor. Even if you're not personally feel affected by it, the person doing the bullying is likely bullying others who are being affected.

Sadly, many teens don't speak up when they're being cyber bullied because they're afraid it will make them appear weak or that sharing it will embarrass them even more.

Bullying is not limited to social media.

Bullying can happen at school, over the phone or anywhere. It's never ok for anyone to constantly harass you or make you feel uncomfortable in any way. If this happens, be sure to let someone know so that it is addressed right away. Don't worry about what people might think of you for speaking up.

Remember, you could be saving your life or the life of someone else. If you are bullying someone, put a stop to it right away! You might be bullying someone because you don't like the person, or simply because everyone else is doing it. Regardless of how you might feel about a person, harassment is never ok. If you find yourself in a situation where your friends or classmates are bullying someone, don't engage. Instead, let them know that their behavior is hamful and unnecessary.

Each of us deserves the freedom to pursue our own version of happiness. No one deserves to be bullied.
- Barack Obama

- Scenario I:

There's a girl at school that no one seems to like because she has a bad attitude. You have also had experiences with her that haven't been very pleasant. You notice on one of your social media pages that all of your friends begin to circulate nasty messages about her and her family. They also tag you so that you can chime in.

What do you do?

_____
_____
_____
_____
_____
_____
_____
_____
_____
_____
_____
_____

- Scenario II:

You receive a direct message on one of your social media pages from a guy you don't recognize. He says he's seen you around and thinks you're cute. You view his profile pictures and think he's cute, too. He wants to get to know you and asks if you want to meet up so that you can hang out. What do you do?

What do you do?

- Self-Reflection II:

- *What do you like most about social media? What about social media irritates you most?*

- *Have you ever been bullied on social media or elsewhere? How did you handle it? What could you have done differently?*

- *Have you ever been contacted by a guy you didn't know through social media who wanted to meet up? How did you handle it?*

_____

_____

_____

_____

_____

_____

_____

_____

_____

_____

_____

Social Media: What's The Big Deal? - Assignment I:

- *Take a look at your social media pages this week and pay attention to the comments of your friends and followers. Make a list of any friends who appear to consistently make negative or embarrassing comments about other people. Commit to having a conversation with these friends about why this makes you uncomfortable by the end of the week. If they continue to demonstrate the same behavior, commit to blocking or unfollowing these friends by the end of the week.*

Remember to report any comments that lend themselves to harassment or threats.

Always have eyes that sees the best in people, a heart that loves and forgives, a mind that forgets the bad, and a soul that never loses faith in what's possible

Dating, Love and Committed Relationships: What Does it All Mean?

At this stage, you're curious about love and relationships. This is completely normal for any teenager.

You're curious about how you feel about other people and how other people feel about you. This is especially true when it comes to liking and getting to know a guy. So, how does it all work?

Is there a magic formula for establishing a relationship and, eventually, love? 'What does love look like, and how do you know if it's real? There is no magic formula for love and relationships. However, there are key foundational concepts that can help to navigate you on your journey.

Dating: The Point of It All

At this age, you might be interested in dating. If you're not ready to date, you might be interested in what it means to date. Dating is all about getting to know someone over time so that, eventually, you can decide if it's a person you'd like to enter into a long-term relationship with.

Going out on a date with someone does not mean that you have to be committed to them.
It simply means that you're interested in getting to know more about them—their background, interests, likes and dislikes. It's also a great opportunity to explore what you have in common.

It's a good idea to let the person you're dating know that you're simply getting to know him, and that he might not be the only person you choose to date. This will help to eliminate any misconception that he's the only person you're seeing. Unfortunately, many people use "dating" and "committed relationships" interchangeably. However, the two should not be confused.

Dating is the "getting to know you" phase, whereas a committed relationship is the "we're seeing each other and no one else phase". This might also be solidified by giving each other titles, such as "boyfriend" and "girlfriend".

Put yourself first. Say No, it's not selfish. It is necessary

What If I'm Asked Out On A Date?

How do you know when a guy is asking you out on a date? Most guys don't use the term "date" anymore when they're asking you out. Many times, they'll simply ask if you want to hang out with them. If he's wanting to spend time with you in a way that isn't inappropriate, he's likely interested in getting to know you.

Don't be shy to ask questions about what his intentions are to make sure you're both on the same page. What should you do if a guy asks you out on a date? Start by deciding whether or not you're interested in getting to know him more.

If the answer is yes, let your parent or guardian know that you'd like to spend some time with him, and find out whether or not they think it's ok for you to do so.

If the answer is yes, make sure that your parent or guardian knows who you are going out with. It's best that your parent or guardian actually meets your date before you go out.

It's also important that your parent or guardian knows where you're going. If anything were to happen to you, they need to know who you're with and where you are.

Where Should We Go?

Choose a place that is safe and that you'll both enjoy. For example, your date should not be at his house alone. You might be tempted to engage in sexual activity if you're at his house (or yours) with no one around.

Public places that allow you to have fun while getting to know one another are always a great idea.

This might include the movie theatre and your favorite food place afterward, the bowling alley, an arcade or a concert. Remember, the point of dating is to get to know one another's personalities.

What If I'm Not Interested?

What if you're asked on a date but you're not interested? This happens a lot, and it's okay. Just be sure to be honest with the guy who has asked you out by letting him know that you appreciate that he's interested, but you're not interested in a dating him right now.

Be careful not to be rude or inconsiderate of his feelings by pointing out his flaws. Like you, guys have emotions, and harsh words can damage their self-esteem.

It's possible to say "no" and be kind.

What If I'm Uncomfortable with Dating?

Maybe a guy has asked you out on a date but you're not comfortable with dating yet. That's ok! You can take it as slow as you need to. Try getting to know him more over the phone or at school as just friends. If this isn't possible, group dating might be an option.

This is when you invite other friends along with you on a date so that it feels less awkward for you. Group dating might also make you feel a lot safer.

What If My Parents and I Don't See Eye to Eye About Dating?

You might be in a situation where you want to go out on a date but your parents are not comfortable with you dating yet. This is perfectly normal. Many parents set age limits on dating based on when they feel their teens are mature enough to go out with a guy on their own. This is because they know the dangers of dating before being mature enough to handle the responsibility that comes with it.

Dating comes with responsibility.

It means being strong enough to say "no" when necessary. It means being accountable for what time you return home. It means being aware of your surroundings at all times and recognizing if you're in the presence of possible danger.

You might think your parents are being unreasonable, but they love and care for you more than you know. They'd much prefer that you focus on school at this age because boys can be a major distraction. Talk to your parents about when they think you might be ready to date and what their expectations are.

Trust that your parents will support you in dating when the time is right. When that time comes, make sure you keep them in the loop about your dating experiences. They want to support you in all areas of your life; dating is no exception. You'll find that they have very good insight if you're willing to open up and share. Sharing about your dating life with your parents is also a great way to bond.

Remember people love to bring up your past, when they're threatened by your present.

What Is LOVE?

Love is having a deep affection for someone that comes naturally and is unconditional.

Love is much like oxygen. We all need it to survive. Oxygen comes to us naturally. We don't have to create it. Oxygen is always available to us, whether we're up, down, right or wrong. Oxygen is available to us unconditionally and is everlasting. It gives without ever expecting anything in return.

It is very easy to confuse love with emotions that are driven by hormones as a teenager.

For example, maybe you've been talking to or spending time with a guy who you really like, and you feel that he really likes you. When he comes around, you might get nervous or feel "butterflies". You might get excited when you see him or hear his voice. You might even find yourself thinking of him often when he's not around.

This might mean that you're very attracted to him or really like him, but it doesn't necessarily mean that you're in love with him. Some refer to this as "puppy love". It's a phrase people use to describe emotions that mimic love during an early stage of a relationship.

Keep in mind that you haven't truly invested any of your livestogether to know that what you're experiencing is actually love. Your only point of reference is how you feel, but love is more than just a feeling.

Introducing sex into a dating relationship because you think you're in love is never a good idea.

Remember, sex can produce hormones that send bonding signals to the brain. This makes it difficult to convince yourself that what you're experiencing is anything but love, when in reality, what you're really experiencing is a longing for the bond or feelings of affection that you've now associated with having sex.

This is a concept referred to as lust, not love.

If a guy tries to convince you that you don't love him if you refuse to have sex, he doesn't understand love to begin with. He's putting his wants and needs before yours, which is not a demonstration of love at all.

He might even try to hurt you with words out of frustration. Don't ever let anyone convince you that sex or any form of mental of physical abuse is a form of love. Emotional or physical abuse is never ok.

If this happens, distance yourself from that person right away and let your parent or mentor know.

Real love is unselfish.

Your parents, for example, have a deep affection for you that they probably will never be able to put into words. But, beyond just the feeling, they would do anything for you, regardless of whether or not you're deserving of it. They also have a natural desire to make sure that you're happy and provided for, even before their own happiness and needs.

Can you honestly say that you care more about another person's happiness and needs than your own? Can you honestly say that you'd still care deeply about a person, even if they badly hurt your feelings?

Could you put someone before yourself without even expecting it in return? It takes a certain level of maturity to really love someone. Most importantly, loving someone else requires that you first understand and love yourself.

You're certainly not expected to fully understand how to love someone as a teenager. You have your entire life to find the person you want to love for the rest of your life.

For now, focus on understanding who you are and preparing yourself for the future.

What Is A Committed Relationship?

A committed relationship is one where you and the person you're dating decide to remain in a relationship with just each other. At this point, you both feel you've gathered all the information you need from one another to know that you have shared interests, love one another, and see a future together long-term.

In most cases, couples who enter into a committed relationship have an ultimate goal of marriage. You're not likely planning to get married anytime soon, so entering into a committed relationship as a teenager is probably too soon. You still have a lot to learn about yourself as you continue to mature before you can truly commit yourself to anyone else.

Dealing with Heartbreak?

Even if you're just dating and haven't entered into a committed relationship, it's easy for your emotions to become involved. This is especially true if someone you really like has done something to hurt your feelings. Feelings of sadness and even anger are normal when you're hurt by someone you care about.

However, never blame yourself for anyone else's actions. Teen girls have a tendency to find fault in themselves when someone has done something to hurt them. They begin to tell themselves that they aren't good enough, popular enough, pretty enough or smart enough. Don't fall into this trap. You are perfect just the way you are.

If you experience "heartbreak", remind yourself that you are amazing, despite the other person's faults. Also, focus on things you love to do, rather than spending time replaying what went wrong or trying to figure out what you could have done differently.

Eventually, you'll get past your feelings of hurt, but you have to learn to let it go. The more you hold onto your hurt, the longer it will take for you to move past it. If you find that trying to move past your hurt is too difficult, talk to your parent or mentor so that they can help guide you through it.

The past is where you learned the lesson. The future is where you apply the lesson.

Dating, Love and Committed Relationships: What Does It All Mean? Scenario I

A guy that attends your school asks you out on a date. Your parents say it's ok that you go to the movies with him. When you get to the movies, he tells you he wants to leave and go over to his house and watch a movie instead. His house is not far and there's no one home. He promises to have you back at the movie theater in time for your parents to pick you up.

What do you do?

Dating, Love and Committed Relationships: What Does It All Mean? Scenario II

A guy that you really like tells you he's into you and asks you if you've ever had sex. You tell him no and he begins to laugh. He tells you that he doesn't date girls who can't prove to him that they're really into him. He promises to be gentle and not to tell anyone. He finds it hard to believe that you're into him if you're not willing to try anything with him at all. You talk to your girlfriends about it and they tell you how lucky you are that he likes you because so many other girls are into him. He even begins to send you sexually explicit text messages.

What do you do?

_____

_____

_____

_____

_____

_____

_____

_____

_____

Dating, Love and Committed Relationships: What Does It All Mean? Scenario III

You've been talking to a guy at school who wants to know if you can hang out over the weekend. When you bring it up to your parents, they disapprove. You become frustrated because you don't understand why your parents won't allow you to spend time with him. The guy suggests that you tell your parents you're going to the mall with your friends so that the two of you can meet up. He tries to convince you that your parents don't trust you and that you're old enough to make your own decisions

What do you do?

_____
_____
_____
_____
_____
_____
_____
_____
_____
_____

Dating, Love and Committed Relationships: What Does It All Mean? Self-Reflection

- Are you currently dating or thinking about dating? What about dating interests you most?

- Have you ever felt like you were in love but realized you weren't? How did you know the difference? How would you describe love compared to lust?

- ∆ Have you ever been hurt by a guy that you really cared about? How did you handle it? How could you have handled it differently?

What do you do?

_____
_____
_____
_____
_____
_____
_____
_____
_____
_____
_____
_____

Dating, Love and Committed Relationships: What Does It All Mean? Assignment:

Make a list of all the characteristics that resemble love to you. Describe how dating can help you determine whether or not a person has these characteristics. Then, describe how a dating relationship would differ from a committed relationship.

My Mission:
To be so busy loving my life that I have no time
for hate, regret, worry, fret or fear.
Loubis and Champaigne

What if I'm Not Sure About My Sexual Orientation?

Your sexual orientation can affect your dating life and self-esteem.

If you're unsure about whether you're attracted to guys or girls, this might make you extremely uncomfortable or even frustrated. This simply means you're still trying to figure out your sexual orientation—whether you like the same sex or opposite sex.

If you're attracted to the same sex, you might be gay or lesbian (also referred to as homosexual). If you're attracted to both girls and guys, you might be bisexual.

This doesn't mean that anything is wrong with you, and you shouldn't be afraid.

Many teens begin to notice differences in their sexual orientation from that of their peers during this stage. It might take several more years of learning about yourself, including your dating experiences, before you truly understand your sexual orientation.

If you're unsure about your sexual orientation or you know that you are gay, lesbian or bisexual, it's important that you talk to someone. This can be your parents, mentor and/or a friend that you trust. You might be afraid that sharing these feelings might result in people teasing or judging you because not everyone is accepting of homosexuality.

However, hiding who you truly are and living in fear can lead to high stress, anxiety and depression. This is why having a strong support system is so important

Forgive
Life becomes easier when you learn to accept the apology you never got.
-R. Brault

Dealing With My Parents' Divorce

Your parents are getting a divorce or are divorced. Whether this is expected or unexpected, it is a traumatizing and overwhelming event to experience. Sometimes, teens and children feel like they somehow caused the divorce. However, it is important to remember that it is not your fault.

Divorce occurs because of problems between the parents. You will have a lot of feelings regarding the divorce and it is important to speak with another adult or a counselor. Keeping your feelings bottled up can lead to depression, anxiety, use of alcohol, drugs, pills to numb the pain and feeling you might be feeling.

No matter how old you might be, facing your parents' divorce is never easy. As a teenager, it can be even more challenging. Your emotions may already be running all over the place with everything you have going on at school, with friends, or in your own relationships. Yet the situation in your home may only add to or amplify the stress you're already feeling.

When dealing with your parents' divorce as a teenager, do your best to stay positive. Your parents may have divorced because they were not happy together, so now living apart might help them achieve the happiness that they deserve. Face the tough emotions you're experiencing so that they don't get the best of you. Stay focused on your strengths and your goals for the future. You can do it.

If you're dealing with your parents' divorce as a teenager, remember important points and facts to help you cope with this situation.

It was never your fault - Witnessing the end of your parents' relationship can be one of the hardest things you'll have to go through, but never forget that it wasn't your fault. Relationships are complicated, no matter how long people have been together. Parents separate because of issues that are just between them. You and the things you've done or haven't done didn't cause their separation.

Don't let anger get the best of you - The anger you feel towards your parents for not staying together can affect you greatly. It is okay to feel angry, but try to remember not to let it control you or impact your life for the worse. Keep up with school and other any work, and stay involved with the activities you love to do. If you are feeling frustrated with friends or peers in ways you hadn't before, remember that it might not be them you are frustrated at.

Take a breath and move forward. Be fair to yourself and to those around you by not letting anger get the best of you.

Don't be their go-between - Sometimes, parents want their children to send messages for them between homes. Know that this is not your responsibility. Your parents should have a handle on how they plan to manage their communication without involving you. Let them know that it is difficult for you to be the messenger between, so it will be better they call each other or text each other.

What are some emotions I may feel after the divorce?

Shock – especially if you were not expecting the divorce

Anger – either directed at your parents or at no one specifically.

Sadness –

Guilt – you feel like the divorce is your fault.

Anxiety – worrying about the future and who is going to take care of you.

Worry – you feel that in the future you will get divorced.

Fear – afraid of losing a parent.

Embarrassed – you do not want people to know that things in your family are changing.

Loneliness – no one understands you or understands what you are going through.

Relieved – there is now less tension at home

Talk to your parents - Don't keep your parents in the dark about how you are feeling. Let them know what you're experiencing emotionally throughout as your family faces changes. It's okay to tell your parents that you are angry or sad, even if you think that might make them feel bad. They are there for you and want to know how you are doing.

Talk to them about how things are going today and let them know what you want for your family as you all move forward. Betting on your parents getting back together in the future may not be an outcome to count on, but desiring happiness and well-being for everyone, plus a friendly standing between your two homes, are goals that many families can achieve.

Talk to your close friends - The people that love you go farther than just your family. Your close friends care about you and want to know how you are feeling or what is bothering you. Even though it might be hard to talk about with some friends, don't keep your close ones in the dark. Tell them what is going on and how you are feeling. Their support during this difficult transition could be an outstanding help to you.

Talk to an expert - This might be something you feel uncomfortable with at first, but it can truly be a huge help. If you're having a hard time managing your emotions—even if you are talking to your parent and your friends—there are other people who can help. Your school counselor or a local therapist can be great people to talk to during tough times. They may even provide you with helpful insights and tips for managing your emotions.

What else can I do to make dealing with divorce easier?

Be fair to both parents: Do not "take sides" and if your parents are persuading you to pick their side, tell them you do not want to. You need to be able to openly talk to or be with a parent without the other getting angry or jealous.

Work it out: it will not be easy to coordinate both parents coming to one of your events or games. Sometimes parents feel awkward going to events when the other parent is there. For example, you have a big soccer game this weekend. Both your parents want to come and you want both parents there. You could organize for your mom to come for the first half and for your dad to come for the second half.

Stay in touch: If you have to alternate time between your mom's house and your dad's house it can be hard on the other parent. Or if your dad takes you on a two-week vacation with him, your mom is going to miss you. Send her a postcard letting her know you miss her and are thinking of her. Or, at home, send her an e-mail asking her how her day was.

Don't worry about the future: talk to your parents about your concerns. If you are worried that their divorce might ruin your future plans, let them know about it, and together you can come up with a solution.

Keep living your life: Sometimes a divorce can make you feel like you have to put your life on hold to deal with your parents' problems – but you need to live your life. Do what you love to do and if you need support, lean on your friends, other family members, and trusted adults. If there is too much tension at home, see if you can stay with a close friend or relative until things get straightened out.

Finally – focus on the positive: divorces happen because parents are not happy with each other anymore. So the result of the divorce might mean that your parents are happier and maybe even have more time to spend with you. You will also learn to cope with tough circumstances and become stronger, which will help you later in life

 You should never rip yourself into pieces to keep others whole. Be You

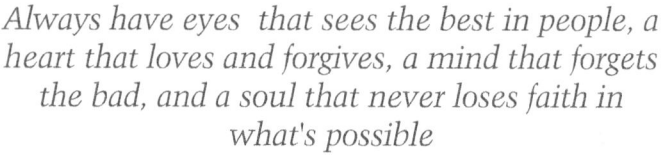
Always have eyes that sees the best in people, a heart that loves and forgives, a mind that forgets the bad, and a soul that never loses faith in what's possible

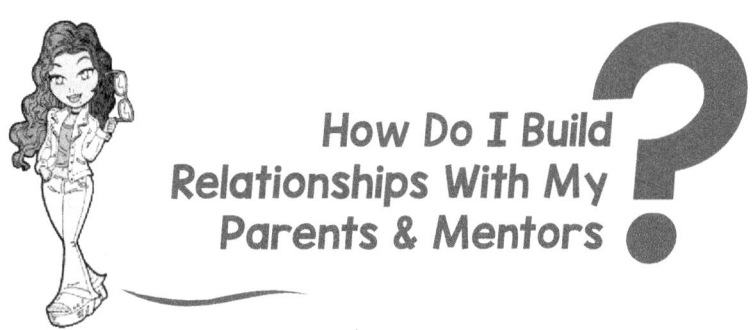

How Do I Build Relationships With My Parents & Mentors?

Some teens find it increasingly harder to connect with their parents as they get older.

This isn't true for all teens. In fact, many teens consider their parents their best friends. Hopefully, this is your experience.

However, if you struggle to connect with your parents or become unsure about how to approach them about topics that are uncomfortable for you, keep in mind that they love you and want to help guide you through whatever you're going through.

Asking Questions and Taking Advice

It can be hard to open up to your parents sometimes because you're afraid that they might become upset or judge you. Many times, this is far from the case. Parents are so eager to have you open up to them, they'd rather listen to you and try to help out of love than to lash out on you and push you away.

Don't be afraid to approach your parents about anything.

Even if your parents become visibly upset by a topic you approach them with, keep in mind that they have a natural instinct to protect you out of love. This parental instinct might cause them to react with heightened emotions.

This doesn't mean they don't love you or want to have tough conversations with you. Even your parents are still learning. In this case, they're learning how to adjust to your changing needs and lifestyle.

Some parents might also be experiencing struggles of their own that make it harder for them to be fully present at times. Don't let this keep you from asking them questions and sharing information about what you're experiencing. Be patient with your parents, even when the conversations are tough.

Let them know you appreciate them for listening, even if they don't have all the answers. It's important that you support each other through this phase of transition and work together to find solutions.

When your parents give you advise, listen!

No one's perfect—not even your parents, but your parents were certainly teenagers once and have a lot of very valuable wisdom. They have information and personal experiences that your friends couldn't dream of giving you, so take in everything you can get from your parents and put it to use. You'll be glad you did!

What Are Mentors For?

You might already have a mentor who you talk to regularly. If you do, you know how nice it is to talk with an adult about anything without feeling afraid or judged. Examples of mentors might be teachers, aunts, after-school workers or church leaders.

Mentors are not meant to replace your parents. However, they can provide your parents with additional support by being a listening ear and giving you resources you need to successfully transition into young adulthood.

In There will always be someone who can't see your worth. Don't let it be you

How Do I Build Relationships with My Parents and Mentors? Scenario:

You are experiencing feelings about several things that you don't really understand. You've talked with your friends about it but you know that they're still trying to figure it all out, just like you. You want to talk to your parents about it but you've never really talked to them about personal matters before, and you're not sure about how they'll respond.

What do you do?

How Do I Build Relationships with My Parents and Mentors? Self-Reflection:

Δ What are some things you've talked to you parents or mentors about in the past that have made you feel confident or safe? (This can be about anything).

Δ What are some reasons why you are uncomfortable talking with your parents or mentors about certain things?

Δ Why might the advice of your parents or mentors be more valuable than the advice of your friends?

_____
_____
_____
_____
_____
_____
_____
_____
_____
_____
_____
_____
_____
_____

How I Do Build Relationships with My Parents and Mentors? Assignment:

Δ Make a list of at least three things you'd like to talk with your parents or mentors about that you haven't been comfortable with discussing before now. Describe why discussing these three things are important to you. Commit to discussing at least one of these things with your parents (and a mentor, if you choose). Be sure to explain the importance of the discussion using your notes.

_____

_____

_____

_____

_____

_____

_____

_____

_____

_____

_____

_____

_____

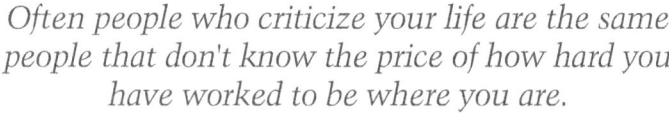

Often people who criticize your life are the same people that don't know the price of how hard you have worked to be where you are.

What About My Personal Goals?

One way to avoid many of the distractions that might negatively affect you as a teen is to set your sights on the goals that you have for yourself. If you focus on your goals and make it a point not to let anything get in your way, you are bound for success!

Your personal goals can be as big or as small as you want them to be, as long as they're meaningful to you.

What Is A Personal Goal?

Personal goals are goals that you set for yourself. No one else can set them for you. These are things that you someday want to accomplish for yourself and dream of achieving. This can be something you hope to accomplish by next month or within the next 5 years.

Examples of personal goals might include achieving a certain number of steps per day, learning how to speak another language, being accepted into the college or your choice, or becoming a professional in your dream line of work.

Setting goals might sound like a simple concept, but it takes discipline to complete the necessary steps to achieve them. It's not enough to say you want to achieve something without actually taking actions toward making it happen.

Being Accountable for Your Goals

Describing specific steps to achieving your goal and setting a timeline are important.

This helps you to be accountable for the goals you've set for yourself. For example, if your goal is to drink more water but you only drink one glass a day, you haven't taken the necessary steps to achieve your goal. You weren't specific in telling yourself how many glasses of water you want to drink per day and for how long.

A better goal would have been to drink more water by having at least 8 glasses a day every day for the next three months. Now, you can take notes on how many glasses of water you've had, where you're lacking, and how close you are to achieving your goal of drinking more water.

Monitoring your goals doesn't require any type of formal tracking process.

There's no need to develop fancy charts or create calculated measures. Make it fun! Track your goals in a way that will keep you engaged. This can be in the form of a colorful checklist you create in your favorite notebook, you can use colorful stickers, or even create a vision board with pictures that reflect your goals.

If you choose to use a vision board, try using colorful pins or clips to demonstrate your progress. You can keep your vision board on your wall or mirror so that it's always there to remind you of what you want to achieve.

The more motivated you are about achieving your goal, the less likely you are to get distracted with temptation.

Tracking your goals helps to motivate you even more. Teens with no goals in mind are more likely for fall victim to many of the peer pressures that can jeopardize their future.

Sometimes, we set goals for ourselves that we don't always achieve. That's ok—don't be too hard on yourself! What matters if that you're working toward you goal. Failures and mistakes can often times help us to understand what to avoid or do more of in order to achieve what we've set out to do.

It doesn't mean you're not good enough or smart enough to be successful. Just stay focused and make the necessary adjustments so that you hit your target the next time.

Tips for Achieving Your Goals

Here are a few tips to help you set your goals and work toward them:

- Stay true to yourself. Don't set goals based on what others think you should do.

- Believe in yourself. You can do anything you set your mind to.

- Make your goals achievable. Try not to set the bar so high that you set yourself up for failure. Start small and gradually expand upon the goals you have for yourself.

- Don't rush. Be diligent and take your time.

- Adjust plans for achieving your goals when necessary. It's ok to make changes.

- Stay committed. Don't back out of a goal that you've set for yourself because you miss the mark a few times.

- Share your goals with family and friends so that they can support you. If your friends make fun of your goals, they are not friends who have your best interest in mind. Surround yourself with friends who are positive and supportive.

Setting Personal Goals - Scenario:

Erica has tried to bring up her score in math for the past two semesters but seems to achieve the same letter grade. She studies often but is easily distracted by the television and her phone. She also gets bored very quickly when working on math. She has a major test coming up that could potentially improve her overall score. Describe a goal that Erica can put in place for herself.

What can Erica do to be accountable for achieving this goal?

_____
_____
_____
_____
_____
_____
_____
_____
_____
_____
_____

Setting Personal Goals: Self-Reflection

- *What are some personal goals you'd like to achieve? Describe why these goals are important to you.*

- *Have you ever set a goal for yourself that you didn't achieve? How did it make you feel? What could you have done differently?*

Setting Personal Goals: Assignment

Choose one of the goals you described as part of your self-reflection. Write down things you can do to achieve this goal. Describe how you would hold yourself accountable for doing these things. Describe things you can you do to keep yourself motivated. Share this goal with your parents, mentor or a friend.

_____

_____

_____

_____

_____

_____

_____

_____

_____

_____

_____

_____

_____

_____

Affirmational Thoughts & next steps

- *Now that you've completed this book, write down some positive thoughts you have about your teenage journey. What are you feeling more confident or optimistic about?*

- *What are your biggest takeaways? Place a sticky note on the pages that correlate with these takeaways as a reminder that you have a resource handy if a similar situation presents itself. Share your takeaways with a friend..*

_____

_____

_____

_____

_____

_____

_____

_____

_____

_____

_____

_____

_____

Let's Connect

Join Dr. Stem on Face Book Live on Tuesday evenings for discussions on topics discussed in this book and more.

Enroll in Teen Empowerment Webinars and online courses, and connect with other teenagers around the world for moral support, fun and encouragement. All online programs are on:
https://www.drstemmie.com/

Look out for the Parent & Teen Empowerment Conference or Workshop coming to your city, a city near you or at sea.
Inquire at drstem14@gmail.com

About The Author

Originally from Zimbabwe, Southern Africa, **Dr. Sithembile "Stem"Mahlatini** is president and owner of **Global Counseling & Coaching Services,** in Orlando, Florida, and she is also president and founder of Parent & Teen Empowerment Conference & Parent & Teen Empowerment Seminars.

She is a certified life-career coach, author, licensed psychotherapist and motivational/inspirational speaker. She resides in Orlando, Florida USA.

Dr. Stem's life's work is to inspire, motivate and educate others through her books, seminars, workshops, and Counseling and Coaching Services.

Drawing on her background as a licensed psychotherapist, life- career coach, speaker and author, she offers people practical advice on how to tap into their limitless power to change their lives, overcome roadblocks and aspire to be better than the circumstances that surround them.

Her life-long goal is to continue to empower and inspire

teenagers, parents, and couples to be winners at home, work and business. Her motto is, "Each day is an opportunity to change your life and bring out the new you."

Dr. Mahlatini attended Nova Southeastern University where she earned a doctorate degree in education, specializing in organizational leadership. She is also a graduate of Boston University, where she earned a master's degree in social work, and she is licensed as a psychotherapist in Massachusetts and Florida.

She is a member of the Back Talk Toastmasters club, the Professional Woman Network, and the National Association of Social Workers.

Listen to DrStem weekly on The DrStem Show on https://americaoutloud.com/show/the-drstem-show/
Watch DrStem on The DrStem Show on Youtube for inspiration, encouragement and motivation through the interviews she conducts on the show, https://www.youtube.com/results?search_query=drstem+show

In addition to speaking and training, she counsels and coaches clients in her private practice offices in Altamonte Springs, Skype and telephonically. She serves clientele throughout the United States, Africa, the Caribbean, the United Kingdom, and Australia through one-on-one telephone coaching services.

Dr. Stem is available as a trainer and speaker for onsite trainings, groups, and one- on-one coaching for parents, teenagers, women and organizations. Consultations are conducted by telephone or on-site. Her programs include:

- Bridging the Gap Between Parents and Teenagers
- Pampering The "Princess Within"
- Overcoming Being All Things to All People
- Possibilities – Turning Dreams into Reality
- Free at Last – Setting Boundaries
- How to Deal with Toxic People
- 15 Strategies to Achieve Your Dream
- How to Live a Simpler Life
- Living a New Life of Confidence- Developing A Healthy Self Esteem
- Taking Charge of Your Life, Money and Family
- Change Your Thinking – Change Your Life
- The Rollercoaster Ride Is Over! Handling Emotions
- Handling Stress: Sink, Swim or Float & MoreBook

Dr. Stem Mahlatini as your next motivational/inspirational speaker for your women's retreat, church, youth retreat, seminar, school assembly, or Business Management–Employee event.

Training, Individual and Group Life Coaching

Contact Dr. Stem Mahlatini at: PHONE: (781) 254-1602

Dr. Stem authored/co-authored the following titles:

1. Beyond the Tears-Bruised but Not Broken- Author Biography-A story of Hope & Encouragement
2. The Power of Prayer & Belief
3. It's Time to Shift -From Fear to Faith
4. Finding Your True Self
5. Emotional Wellness for Women vol. 1
6. Emotional Wellness for Women vol. II
7. Emotional Wellness for Women vol. III
8. The Baby Boomer's Handbook for Women
9. The Power of God
10. Celebration of Life-Inspiration for Women
11. How to Survive When Your Ship Is Sinking: Weathering Life's Storms
12. Beyond the Scars: Real Life Accounts for Women Who Overcame Adversity
13. Confident not Corky: Why self-esteem is Key to a Successful Life, Business and Career

14. Unstoppable: A woman's Guide to Self-confidence book and workbook.
15. Zero Limits: A Teenager's Guide to Life's choices
16. 47 1/2 Things to Say to Your Teenager and How to Say Them
17. 47 1/2 Things Teenagers Need to Know About Getting Along with Their Parents
18. CDC- Courage Determination Confidence: A Teenager's Handbook to Socially Acceptable Life Skills
19. 365 Daily Success & Motivation Doses for Teens
20. 50; A celebration of Life Lessons
21. Dose of Motivation & Encouragement for Teachers
22. Profits are Better than Wages: The key to Living Your Dreams
23. Finding your True Self – Bringing Clarity and Purpose to Your Life
24. Respect- Connecting with Disconnected Students: Seven Steps to Reach the Students You Teach
25. The Blessings of Being a Woman: Embracing Womanhood
26. Build Confidence, Achieve Success
27. Success within reach: reconditioning your paradigm

www.ingramcontent.com/pod-product-compliance
Lightning Source LLC
Chambersburg PA
CBHW052051070526
44584CB00017B/2127